JAPANESE MUNICIPAL GOVERNMENT

WITH AN ACCOUNT OF THE

ADMINISTRATION OF THE CITY OF KOBE.

BY

J. TWIZELL WAWN

(Of Her Britannic Majesty's Consular Service, Japan).

———:o:———

Kobe:

Office of the "Kobe Chronicle."

1899.

In the interest of creating a more extensive selection of rare historical book reprints, we have chosen to reproduce this title even though it may possibly have occasional imperfections such as missing and blurred pages, missing text, poor pictures, markings, dark backgrounds and other reproduction issues beyond our control. Because this work is culturally important, we have made it available as a part of our commitment to protecting, preserving and promoting the world's literature. Thank you for your understanding.

JAPANESE MUNICIPAL GOVERNMENT.

BY

J. TWIZELL WAWN

(*Of Her Britannic Majesty's Consular Service, Japan*).

ALTHOUGH this report is intended chiefly to deal with the internal administration of *shi* or cities, it may be as well to glance first at the general scheme of provincial administration in Japan.

Previous to the Revolution of 1868, the country was divided into *han* or daimiates, ruled by a *daimio* as by a feudal lord, with little or no responsibility to the Central Government. In 1871 the first step in the path of reform was taken, the *han* were abolished and replaced by *ken* or prefectures; and although in many cases the chiefs of the defunct clans were made governors of the *ken*, they were shorn of all their former state, and the reins of government soon passed into the hands of new and abler men. In 1871 the number of prefectures was 68, but in 1876 it was reduced to 35. Since then further slight changes have taken place, and the present number is 43, which includes Okinawa ken (the Luchu Islands), at present under a special administration. In addition there are the three *fu* or Imperial cities of Tokyo, Kyoto and Osaka, and the Hokkaido (Yesso). The division of Japan into 73 provinces is merely geographical. At the head of the prefecture is the *chiji* (Governor, or prefect) who is under the orders of the Minister for Home Affairs. Each prefecture possesses a *kenkwai* or prefectural assembly, elected by the inhabitants of the prefecture, which votes supplies and discusses the business of the prefecture generally. In addition there is the *ken sanjikwai* or prefectural council, analogous to the *shi sanjikwai* or city council, the nature and functions of which will be described later on.

A prefecture is divided into *shi* (cities or urban districts) and *gun* (counties or rural districts); *gun* are subdivided into *cho* and *son* (towns and villages), directly under the control of the *guncho*, who is, as it were, governor of the *gun*, and indirectly under that of the governor of the prefecture. Broadly speaking, the distinction between *shi* and *cho* is a distinction of population, *shi* always having more than 25,000 inhabitants; but it is open to the Minister for Home Affairs, on a report from the governor of the prefecture, to refuse the status of *shi* even to a town of over 25,000 inhabitants, if it does not appear fitted to possess the greater measure of autonomy granted to *shi* as opposed to *cho* and *son*. At the present time there are also exceptions in the case of Okinawa prefecture and the Hokkaido, where the *Shisei* (city regulations) have not yet been put into force; but in due time these also will, no doubt, be admitted to the enjoyment of the same privileges as the rest of Japan.

As regards administration there are slight differences between *shi* and *cho-son*, the former enjoying a greater measure of autonomy. It may in especial be noted that in *cho-son* there is no *sanjikwai* or council, the executive power being entrusted to the mayor alone,—possibly because of the difficulty likely to be experienced in finding persons of sufficient ability, possessing at the same time sufficient leisure, to undertake the rather onerous duties of the Council.

In the eye of the law a city is a "juridical person" (*hojin*), possessing certain privileges and charged with certain duties. Citizens also have privileges and duties,—the privilege of taking part in elections, the duty of filling honorary offices, if called upon to do so, unless provided with a reasonable excuse, such, for instance, as illness, old age, or immediately previous service.

CITY ASSEMBLY.

In the exercise of its privileges and discharge of its duties, a city is represented by the *shikwai*, or city assembly, which discusses and decides all questions affecting the city which it is entitled by law to decide.

The number of members is fixed at the following rate:—

In a city of less than 50,000 inhabitants, 30 members.

In a city of more than 50,000 inhabitants, 36 members.

In a city of upwards of 100,000 inhabitants, 3 members are added for every 50,000 in population.

In a city of upwards of 200,000 inhabitants, 3 members are added for every 100,000 in population.

A total of sixty members is the limit. The number of members may be specially varied by city by-laws, but in no case may the limit of sixty be exceeded.

ELECTORS.

Any Japanese householder of or over the age of twenty-five, being a male and possessing public rights (*koken*), who for two years past has been resident within the city and has paid (1) land tax or (2) direct national taxes to the annual amount of two yen or more, is a *shikomin* or citizen, and possesses the right of voting at municipal elections. The stipulation as to two years may be waived by special resolution of the assembly. Persons who have received assistance from the rates may not vote until the lapse of two years from the time when they ceased to receive such assistance. It should be noted that foreigners may be *shijumin*, residents, but not *shikomin*, citizens. It is specially provided that a Japanese possessing public rights may have the right to vote, even though not a citizen, if he pay a larger amount of municipal taxes than one of the three highest citizen tax-payers. This right extends even to women, who, however, may not vote directly, but only through a properly appointed agent. This does not apply to persons whose public rights have been suspended, or to persons serving in the army or navy. Under the above clause a legally constituted company may possess voting rights.

CLASSES OF ELECTORS.

Electors are divided into three classes, according to the proportionate amount of direct municipal taxes paid by them. The division is made in the following manner:—The names on the list of voters being arranged in order of amount of taxes paid, the sums paid by the highest tax-payer are added together until the total is equal to one-third of the total amount of taxes paid by all the electors. The tax-payers who contribute this one-third form the first class of electors. Putting these electors on one side, the sums paid by the highest remaining tax-payers on the list are added together until once more a sum equivalent to one-third of the total amount of taxes paid is reached. These tax-payers form the second class of electors. The remaining tax-payers form the third class. Each class of electors chooses separate representatives on the assembly, but a member need not necessarily belong to the class of electors which he represents.

ELECTORAL DISTRICTS.

In large cities electoral districts or wards may be marked out for convenience in the election of members; and there is no objection to forming districts specially for second or third class elections. The number and boundaries of electoral wards are decided by the assembly; and representatives are allotted to each ward in accordance with the number of electors it contains. The ward to which an elector belongs is decided by his place of residence; if he have no residence within the city, by the situation of the property on which he pays tax and bases his claim to a vote. If an elector pays taxes in more than one ward, he is considered to belong to that ward in which he pays the largest amount.

CANDIDATES.

Any citizen possessing electoral rights may become a candidate for membership of the city assembly, unless he be an official of the prefecture, salaried city official, police or prosecuting officer, priest or minister of any sect or religion, or an elementary school teacher. Other officials must obtain the consent of their superior before they can present themselves for election. Father and son, or brother and brother may not hold seats at the same time. Should two such relatives be elected, the one with the larger number of votes takes the seat; if the votes are equal, the elder candidate is preferred.

Members of the city assembly are unsalaried, and hold office for six years. Elections are triennial, half of the members representing each class retiring every three years. Thus a perpetual fund of at least three years' experience on the part of half of the assembly is assured. Retiring members may be re-elected, but cannot be compelled to serve if they are unwilling to do so. Should a member die, or retire for any reason during his term of office, it is not usual to hold a special election; but the vacancy is filled at the next general election. But a special election may be held, if it is deemed expedient by the city council or by the governor of the prefecture. In such case the member elected retires after serving for the period which was still remaining to his predecessor.

MANNER OF ELECTION.

The mayor is in charge of all arrangements connected with the elections, and himself acts as returning officer.

Not more than two days before the election is to be held a draft table of voters is drawn up showing the names and capacity of the persons entitled to vote. From this draft the list of voters is compiled. If the city be divided into several electoral wards, there must be a draft table and list for each ward separately. The list of voters must lie at the city office, or some other place, open to the public inspection for a space of at least seven days. During this period claims to be put on the list may be sent in to the mayor. Decision as to electoral rights lies with the city assembly.

The revised list of electors must be finally settled at least ten days before the election is to take place; and no person has the right to vote, unless his name is on this list.

The time and place of the election is fixed by the mayor; and publicly notified, together with the number and class of the representatives to be elected, at least seven days beforehand. Two or four men from among the electors are chosen to act as polling clerks; and if there are electoral wards a returning officer must be appointed for each ward.

Voting is by ballot, the voter reporting his name and address at the time of handing in his vote. The voting paper is placed by the presiding officer in a closed box, which is not opened until after the completion of the poll. Voting by proxy is permitted, but the holder of the proxy must be an independent Japanese subject, possessing public rights. A vote is invalid: (1) if no name is written on it, or the name cannot be read, (2) if it cannot be decided who is the person voted for, (3) if the name of a person ineligible for election is written on it, or (4) if anything is written on it except the name of the person voted for.

The candidate obtaining the majority of valid votes is declared elected. In a case of equality of votes, the elder candidate takes the seat. In case of a further equality of age, the decision is made by drawing lots.

The returning officer must, as soon as possible after the close of the poll, announce the names of the persons elected. If a person elected does not wish to serve, he must notify the mayor within five days. Appeals as to the validity of elections must be made to the mayor within seven days. The result of the election is reported by the mayor to the governor of the prefecture, and all questions as to the validity of elections are decided by the prefectural council. If the election is held to be invalid, the governor may order a new one; in such case the old list of voters is used.

FUNCTIONS OF CITY ASSEMBLY.

The duties and functions of the city assembly may be classified as follows:

1. The framing or amendment of city rules and by-laws.

All questions relating to the affairs of the city, and to the rights and duties of the citizens, may be decided by the assembly, and rules be drawn up accordingly. By-laws may be made concerning city property; but such rules and by-laws must not be contrary to the national law, and must be notified to the public in the manner customary in the locality. The approval of the Minister for Home Affairs is necessary before such rules and by-laws can be put into force.

2. The approval of undertakings the expenses of which are to be borne by the city.

Such, for instance, as expenses in connection with engineering sanitary works, or education, the construction and maintenance of schools, hospitals, water-works, &c. But there is certain other business, to be indicated later on, the transaction of which is entrusted to the mayor by law, and the expenses of which are borne by the city, without the approval of the assembly being necessary.

3. The approval of the yearly estimates, or of further disbursements or receipts beyond or in excess of the estimates.

The yearly estimates are drawn up by the council, in consultation with the heads of the various departments, and then presented for approval to the assembly. If further disbursements become necessary, supplementary estimates are introduced.

4. The adoption of the yearly financial report.

This is also drawn up by the city council, and submitted by them to the assembly.

5. The making of rules for the assessment and levying, when not already fixed by law, of charges paid for the use of city property, of fees, city taxes, and forced labour and contributions.

6. The sale, barter, transfer, pledge or mortgage of city property.

7. All dealings with city capital.

8. The undertaking of burdens or repudiation of rights not already settled by the financial estimates.

9. The drawing up of rules for the supervision of city property and plant.

10. The assessment of the amount of personal security to be deposited by city officials (Revenue officer, &c.).

11. The carrying on of lawsuits on behalf of the city, and arrangements of compromises, &c.

12. The election of city officials.

The assembly has the right to call for and inspect documents relating to the transaction of city business, and to inquire into the manner in which the finances and work generally are carried on. In order to elucidate any point, it may demand a report from the Mayor, and examine vouchers.

The assembly decides all questions which may arise with reference to the existence or non-existence of electoral rights, the correctness of the register of voters and of its division into classes, and the existence of the right to vote by proxy. An appeal from the decision of the assembly may be made to the prefectural council, whence a further appeal lies to the Administrative Court (*Gyosei Saibansho*) in Tokyo.

At the beginning of each year the assembly elects a chairman and vice-chairman to serve for the ensuing twelve months. It may here be noticed that the *gicho*, or chairman of the assembly, is a different person to the *shicho*, or mayor, the latter being a salaried official. Further, in the case of towns and villages (*cho-son*) the mayor is *ex officio* chairman of the assembly in contradistinction to the rule in the case of cities. The chairman may not preside when a question is being discussed in which he himself or one of his near relatives (parent, brother or sister, wife or child) is concerned; in such case his place is taken by the vice-chairman. When there are at the same time similar objections in the case of the latter the oldest member present takes the chair. Members of the council may attend meetings of the assembly, and give explanations relating to the matter under discussion.

The chairman may summon the assembly at the request of the mayor or council, or of more than one-fourth of the members of the assembly. Except in cases of great urgency, at least 3 days' notice must be given of the business to be transacted before the meeting takes place. The usual course is to settle the date at the previous meeting of the assembly. At least half the members must be present to form a quorum; but should it be necessary to summon a meeting a second time to discuss business which has been already postponed once, owing to a quorum not being present, resolutions may be passed at the second meeting whether half the members are present or not. Members are not permitted to take part in the discussion of questions in which they themselves or their near relatives are concerned. If the number of members competent to discuss a matter is thus so reduced that a quorum cannot be obtained, the decision of the question is entrusted to the prefectural council.

The resolutions of the assembly are decided by a majority of votes; if the number of votes be equal, a second decision is taken; if the numbers are still equal a casting vote is given by the chairman. In case of the election of city officers, the voting must be by ballot. The single vote system is to be pursued, and in order to be elected a candidate must obtain more than half of the total votes given. If none of the candidates obtain more than half, those with the two highest number of votes must be taken and a second ballot held to decide between them. If the three highest candidates should have an equal number of votes, two are chosen by lot, and the second ballot held. Or, instead of this form of election, the assembly may proceed by nomination or recommendation, the chairman proposing a candidate for the office, and the assembly approving or disapproving of his choice.

Discussions of the assembly are, as a rule, open to the public; but the chairman may, if he considers it advisable, order hearers to be excluded. The chairman may apportion duties amongst the members, he himself superintending the whole; he opens, closes and adjourns meetings, and preserves order. Should any of the public present at a meeting openly express approval or disapproval of remarks made by members, or become disorderly, the chairman may order their expulsion from the room. In case of illness or absence of the chairman, the vice-chairman presides.

Minutes of the proceedings are taken by a clerk, who records the names of members present at the meeting, and details of resolutions proposed and business transacted. At the close of the meeting these minutes are read aloud, and signed by the chairman and two or more of the members, a copy being subsequently sent to the mayor. The clerk is chosen by the assembly on the chairman's nomination; but in practice a clerk from the city office is appointed to fill the post. The assembly may make rules regarding minutiæ of procedure, &c., ambiguous or left unsettled by law, and impose fines of not more than two yen for infractions thereof.

It will be observed that the mayor in Japan is on a different footing to his namesake in England. In Japan he is the servant of the assembly, instead of being its head, as in England. He is not the leading citizen, but the leading official of the city.

The executive machine of the city is the *sanjikwai* or council, which is composed of the following:—

(1) The *shicho* or mayor.

(2) The *joyaku*: vice or assistant mayor; in Tokyo there are three; in Kyoto and Osaka two each; in other cities one.

(3) *Sanjikwaiin* or councillors; in Tokyo twelve in number; in Kyoto and Osaka nine each; in other cities six. The position is an honorary one.

The number of assistant mayors and councillors may be varied by city by-laws.

APPOINTMENT OF CITY OFFICIALS.

The mayor is a salaried official, and his period of office is six years. The mode of appointment is as follows: three candidates are selected by the city assembly, whose names are reported to the Emperor for decision. If none of the three meet with the Imperial approval a second selection is made. If approval is even then not obtained another selection is made, whilst a special substitute is appointed by the Minister for Home Affairs to fill the office until a final settlement is made. As a matter of practice, the candidate who receives the highest number of votes in the assembly is usually appointed. The amount of the mayor's salary is fixed by the assembly; but the approval of the Minister for Home Affairs is necessary.

The vice-mayor and councillors are elected by the Assembly in the same way as ordinary officials; except that in the case of an equality of votes, the final decision is left to the prefectural council instead of deciding by drawing lots.

The vice-mayor is a salaried official; his period of office is six years. The election must be approved by the Governor of the prefecture. The vice-mayor's salary is fixed by the assembly, but the approval of the governor is necessary. If the latter considers the amount unsuitable the question is referred to the prefectural council. The choice for the office of mayor and vice-mayor is not confined only to inhabitants of the city; but those officials become citizens by the fact of their election.

Members of the council are elected from among citizens of at least 30 years of age; period of office is four years, but retiring councillors hold office until their successors are appointed. One-half of the council retires every two years; but should a vacancy occur at any other term, an election is at once held to fill it. Retiring councillors may be re-elected.

Mayor, vice-mayor, and councillors may not hold any other salaried official post in the city or elsewhere; and no priest of any religion or sect may be a councillor. Father and son, or brother and brother may not be councillors at the same time; and a member of the council who stands in such relationship to a newly-elected mayor must retire at once. Neither mayor nor vice-mayor may during his period of office be chairman or director of a joint-stock company, nor may he carry on any other profession without the consent of the Governor of the prefecture. Mayor or vice-mayor may retire after giving three months' notice; but by so doing forfeit any right which they may otherwise have to a pension or grant.

The *shunyuyaku* or revenue officer is charged with the management of the financial business of the city. The same general rules apply to him as to other officials. The revenue officer is nominated by the council, and elected by the assembly. The appointment must receive the approval of the Governor of the prefecture. He must deposit in the hands of the council a sum of money by way of personal security, the amount of which is fixed by the assembly, generally varying from about 300 yen in a large city to 50 yen in a small one.

Clerks, servants and messengers may be employed in the city office, or wherever necessary, and suitable salaries given to them. The number of such clerks, &c., is decided by the assembly, and appointments are in the hands of the council.

For the sake of convenience in the transaction of municipal business, a city may be divided into several *ku* or wards, if in the opinion of the council such a division is advisable. In cases where there is a ward assembly, it elects the *kucho*, or head of the ward, and his deputy. If there is no ward assembly, the city assembly makes the appointments. The office is limited to citizens possessing electoral rights in the ward or its neighbouring ward. In Tokyo, Kyoto and Osaka, heads of wards and their deputies are chosen by the city council, and may receive salaries; assistants and servants may also be employed if necessary. In other cities heads of wards and their deputies are unsalaried.

COMMITTEES.

The city assembly may appoint special or ordinary committees to deal with particular business.

A committee may consist of
(1) Members of the council only.
(2) Members of the assembly only (with the exception of the chairman of the committee).
(3) Members of the council, together with members of the assembly.
(4) Members of the council and assembly, together with individuals chosen from among citizens possessing electoral rights.

Committee-men from the assembly are elected by the assembly, those from among the council are nominated by the mayor, and those from among the citizens are chosen by the council. In every case a member of the council is made chairman of the committee. Liberty is given to the assembly to make special by-laws as regards the organisation of ordinary committees.

Heads of wards and members of committees may, by resolution of the assembly, be granted a suitable remuneration for their services over and above the amount of expenses actually incurred by them in the discharge of their duties. City officials are eligible for re-election on the expiry of their terms of office. Unless there is any special agreement to the contrary, salaried officials and servants may retire at any time.

FUNCTIONS OF COUNCIL.

The City Council is charged with the executive control of city affairs.

Its duties may be classed as follows :—

1. The preparation of business for the assembly; and the execution of its decisions.

This includes the drafting of bills, and the drawing up of the yearly estimates. If, in the opinion of the council, or of the (prefectural or home) controlling office, a resolution of the assembly is *ultra vires*, contrary to law, contrary to the public advantage, the council may suspend the carrying into effect of the decision, and cause the question to be rediscussed. If the assembly refuses to alter its decision, the matter is referred to the prefectural council, whence a further appeal lies to the Administrative Court in Tokyo.

2. The general control and supervision of city public works; *i.e.* schools, hospitals, water-works, &c. If there is an individual or committee specially appointed to take charge of such property, his or their duties are under the supervision of the council.

3. The general control of the city finances.

The work of the revenue officer is superintended by the council; taxes and fees are collected and disbursements made by its orders, in accordance with the yearly estimates or special resolutions of the assembly.

4. The protection of the privileges of the city and the preservation of its property.

5. Supervision of city officials and servants, and infliction of disciplinary punishment, when necessary, on any official except the mayor. Such punishment may take the form of a reprimand, or a fine may be inflicted to the amount of not more than ten yen. City officials who may be so punished include the assistant mayor, revenue officers, clerks, heads of districts, &c. Disciplinary punishment on the mayor can only be inflicted by the governor of the prefecture.

6. Preservation of public documents and papers.

7. The representation of the city in discussions as to law-suits and their compromise, and in carrying on negotiations.

8. The levying and collection of rents, taxes, fees and forced labour, and contributions, in accordance with the decisions of the assembly.

9. The transaction of any other business with which it may be entrusted by law or by Imperial prefectural decree.

In order to pass a resolution the mayor or vice-mayor, and at least one-third of the members of the council, must be present. In case of an equality of votes the mayor, who presides, has the casting vote. If a resolution of the council should be *ultra vires*, contrary to law, or calculated to injure the common good, the mayor may, on his own initiative, or on receiving orders from the governor or Minister for Home Affairs, suspend its operation and refer the question to the prefectural council. In cases where, owing to members of the council being deterred from taking part in discussion by family relationship to the person concerned, a quorum cannot be obtained, the decision of the question is entrusted to the city assembly.

FUNCTION OF MAYOR.

The mayor is the chief executive official, and controls and supervises the transaction of business. It is his duty to see that the administrative machine works smoothly, that there are no stoppages or accumulations of work. When necessary he summons the council, lays business before them, and carries out the decision arrived at. He conducts and signs all correspondence in the name of the council. He has also other duties, with which he is specially entrusted by law, and in the carrying out of which he acts independently of the city council. In cases of great urgency, when there is no time to summon a meeting of the council, the mayor takes action on his own responsibility, and at the next opportunity reports to the council what he has done.

It is the duty of the city council to aid the mayor in carrying out his work. The mayor may, on obtaining the consent of the assembly, apportion special work to the councillors, on which the assembly may vote to the latter a suitable reward for the duties discharged by them, over and above remuneration for expenses necessarily incurred in the execution of their work.

REVENUE OFFICER.

The revenue officer receives payments made to the city, disburses expenses, and is charged with the conduct of financial business generally.

CLERKS.

Clerks (*shoki*) are under the control of the mayor, and transact business according to his direction.

HEADS OF WARDS.

Heads of wards (*kucho*) and their deputies (*dairisha*) are instruments of the council. They are not directly responsible to the public, but receive their order from the city council, and carry on the administration of their ward accordingly.

COMMITTEES.

Committees are under the control of the council, and are entrusted with the supervision of special public works or branches of the administration. The mayor may at will take the chair or participate in the discussion at any committee meeting.

SPECIAL DUTIES OF MAYOR.

As before mentioned the mayor is entrusted by law with the discharge of certain duties, in which he acts independently of the council. Those duties are as follows:

1. The duties of an auxiliary judicial and police official, and the discharge of local police work entrusted to him by law. These duties are, of course, only discharged by the mayor where there is no local police office to do the work,—a state of things never likely to exist.

2. At maritime places, the work of the *urayakuba*, or local marine office, certain work in connection with the occurrence of wrecks and the assistance of shipwrecked persons.

3. Business belonging to the city in connection with the general administrative system of the prefecture or of the whole country.

Expenses incurred in carrying out these duties are to be borne by the city, without requiring the approval of the assembly.

PENSIONS, &c.

Rules may be made by the assembly permitting the granting of pensions to the mayor, vice-mayor, and other salaried officials on their retirement. If any such retired city official should take an official post under the Government, or serve in a public capacity in any Imperial city, prefecture, rural district, city, town or village, and receive salary for his services, his pension ceases for the time. Should he, in consequence of such services, become eligible for a pension equal to, or in excess of that which he formerly received, he loses all title to the former pension. Disputes as to salaries, pensions, &c., are referred to the prefectural council, whence an appeal lies to the Administrative Court.

FINANCES.

A city, being a juridical person, may own property, and such property must be dealt with for the public advantage. Land and buildings may be leased to individuals, and the income thereby obtained devoted to the public use. If certain persons have by force of ancient custom a right to use any portion of the city property, such right may only be abrogated by the assembly in cases of special necessity. Citizens desiring to obtain the right to use city property (land or buildings) may do so by paying a fixed sum or yearly rent, as decided by the assembly. It is the duty of the assembly to preserve intact city funds and property, and only in cases of absolute necessity should land or houses owned by the city be alienated.

Sale or lease of city property must be by public tender, and the disposal of contracts for work to be done or for goods to be supplied must be decided in the same manner, except in cases where special dispatch is necessary, or the assembly considers it advisable that the matter should be left to the sole decision of the mayor.

It is the duty of the city to defray all necessary expenditure, also any burdens hitherto or hereafter laid upon it by law. Its expenses are to be met by proceeds arising from city property, rents, fees, fines and any other source of income which it may by law possess. If these together are not sufficient to meet the expenditure, city taxes may be levied, or resort be taken to forced contributions of labour and goods.

TAXES.

The Japanese system of local taxation is a complicated one, which could not be thoroughly discussed in this paper. I therefore omit any reference to the classification of taxes, which might well be made the subject of a separate report.

FINES.

Regulations as to the taking of fees and the levying of special taxes may be made by the assembly. Fines of not more than one yen and ninety-five sen (¥1.95) may be levied for infractions of city by-laws. The infliction of fines is in the hands of the council; appeals against its decision must be made to the proper court of justice within fourteen days of receipt of the order for payment of the fine.

LEVYING OF TAXES.

City taxes are leviable on persons who have been residing within the city for three months or longer, and the tax is assessed as from the time when the person first commenced to stay in the city. Even persons who are not resident within the city at all must pay tax in respect of land or houses owned by them within the city, or business carried on at a fixed place in the city. This latter provision applies to companies, but there are exceptions in the cases of Government railroads, and post and telegraph offices.

If a person dwells in two or more cities, towns or villages, his income is considered as being divided into a number of equal parts corresponding to the number of places in which tax is paid, and tax in any one place is levied on one of such parts. Income derived from immovable property—land, houses, &c.—is made an exception to this rule, tax being paid only on the income derived from property actually situated within the city in question.

The payment of city taxes is exempted as regards the following:

1. Land, houses or plant belonging to the central Government, to an Imperial city, prefecture, rural district, city, town

or village, or to a public company, and directly employed for the public use. This includes land occupied by railways, telegraph posts, lighthouses, etc., and by Government offices and courts of justice.

2. Land, houses, or plant belonging to or connected with Shinto or Buddhist shrines, temples, public and official schools and hospitals, and other educational or charitable institutions.

3. Government forests and waste land. But to defray the expenses of undertakings which benefit such forest or waste (barren) land, taxes may be levied on obtaining the consent of the Ministers for Home Affairs and Finance. Also in the case of land being cultivated for the first time, the assembly may remit taxes for a portion of the year.

If there are certain public works the use of which is monopolised by one ward of a city, the burden of the building, repairing, and preservation of such works is laid upon the ward, that is, upon persons residing or possessing property within the ward, and taxes are levied accordingly.

City taxes are assessed from the beginning of the next month to that in which the duty to pay tax commences until the end of the month in which it ceases. If during the financial year, the liability of a particular individual to pay taxes ceases, or changes its character, he must report to the mayor accordingly, and tax is paid as before until the end of the month in which such report is made.

FORCED LABOUR.

In order to carry out public works,—such as the construction of schools, hospitals, &c.,—and to preserve the security of the city,—to extinguish fires, or repair embankments, for example—forced labour or contributions may be levied on city tax payers. Except in cases of great urgency, it is permissible to pay a sum of money in lieu of personal service or contribution of goods, or a representative may be sent in the case of forced labour. As the work to be done is limited to that of the nature usually performed by the coolie class, the average daily wage of coolie labour in the locality is generally taken as the standard in computing the amount of money to be paid in lieu of personal service. The amount of labour demanded from each person may be proportioned to the amount of direct city taxes paid by him. If this standard is not followed, the consent of the prefectural council is necessary to whatever mode of assessment is adopted. The nature of the labour or contribution to be levied is decided by the assembly. But forced labour may only be levied in respect of unskilled labour (not of art, scholarship or handicraft). The distribution of the labour is arranged by the council.

This system of forced labour is of greater importance in the country districts, where, at certain times of the year, the peasants are necessarily without much employment, and it is consequently a great advantage to them to be able to devote their leisure time to such work, and thereby lighten the burden of taxation laid upon them. Such labour is frequently employed in the construction and repair of roads, or, as in the province of Tajima, in keeping the highways clear of snow, which falls at times in such quantities as to render all work in the fields impossible. This usage recalls strongly the *corvée* of feudal France.

NON-PAYMENT OF TAXES.

If a person neglect to pay fines, fees, or city taxes due from him within the prescribed period, the city council may press for payment, an urgency order (*tokusokujo*) being served on the defaulter, for which the by-laws may demand a special fee from him. If payment is still delayed, his goods may be seized and sold by public auction to defray the amount due. If a tax-payer plead lack of funds, the council may delay payment during the current financial year. To delay for a further period beyond the financial year, the consent of the assembly is necessary.

Claims for diminution in amount of, or total exemption from payment of, city taxes must be made to the council within three months of delivery of the assessment order (*fukwareijo*). After the expiry of this period, no claim can be sustained during the current financial year.

Disputes as to the assessment of taxes and the right to use city property are decided by the city council, unless the question involves rights at civil law. Appeals from the decision of the city council may be made to the prefectural council, thence to the administrative court.

PUBLIC LOANS.

In cases of absolute necessity, or in order to obtain a permanent benefit to the city, money may be raised by issuing public loan bonds. When the assembly decides upon the issue of bonds, it must at the same time fix the mode of issue, the rate of interest and the manner of redemption. The redemption must be commenced within three years, and completed within 30 years, of the date of issue. Such means of obtaining money may be resorted to in the face of great calamities caused by fire or earthquake, or in order to build new schools, hospitals, &c, when the citizens are unable to bear the burden of the increased taxation necessary to meet extra expenditure. Before such bonds may be issued the consent of the Ministers for Home Affairs and Finance must be obtained. This does not apply to temporary loans, raised to meet the exigencies of the moment and to be repaid within the same financial year, for the raising of which the consent of the assembly is unnecessary.

YEARLY ESTIMATES.

An estimate of the revenue and expenditure for the coming year should be drawn up by the city council two months before the commencement of each financial year. (This rule does not seem to be always strictly adhered to.) This budget must be approved by the assembly before April 1st, and reported to the Governor of the prefecture. Its main details must also be published in the manner customary in the locality. When the estimates are laid before the assembly, there must be sent with them reports on municipal business and a detailed list of the city property.

If the estimated amounts are found to be insufficient, or extraordinary expenses are incurred during the year, supplementary estimates may be brought forward from time to time and receive the sanction of the assembly. Or a sum may be placed apart in the budget for emergencies, out of which the council may make any necessary disbursements without consulting the assembly. But this fund may not be used for any purpose for which the assembly has already refused a grant.

The city accounts are kept by the revenue officer, who makes disbursements and receives payments under the orders of the city council, and in accordance with the yearly estimates. He is personally responsible for all amounts wrongfully paid out by him.

The city accounts must be examined on a fixed day in each month, and a special audit made at least once a year. The monthly examination may be made by the mayor or vice-mayor, but at a special audit two or more members chosen by the assembly must also be present.

The accounts for the whole year should be drawn up and completed within three months from the end of the financial year. The report, together with all certificates, vouchers, etc., is handed by the revenue officer to the council, the latter carefully examines the accounts, and presents them to the assembly for adoption, adding a report of its opinion. When the yearly accounts have been adopted by the assembly, they are reported to the Governor of the prefecture.

WARD ASSEMBLIES.

If any ward of a city should possess special property of its own, or undertake the burden of constructing public works at its own expense, the prefectural council may, after hearing the opinion of the city assembly, issue a regulation constituting a *kukwai* or ward assembly, to transact all business connected with such property and public works. All rules relating to the construction, etc., of the city assembly, apply, so far as appropriate, to the ward assembly. The executive of a ward is under the supervision of the city council, and the head of the ward takes his instructions from that body.

CONTROL BY SUPERIOR OFFICER.

Generally speaking, the administration of the city is, in the first instance, under the supervision of the governor of the prefecture, and in the second instance, under that of the Minister for Home Affairs. In certain special cases the prefectural council is substituted for the governor.

Appeals against the action or decision of the governor or prefectural council must be made to the Minister for Home Affairs within fourteen days of the receipt of notice of the action or decision taken, and at the same time the ground of appeal must be stated. In those special cases, where the appeal lies to the administrative court, it must be made within twenty-one days. Appeals cannot be made both to the administrative court and to the Minister for Home Affairs. As a general rule, the carrying out of the action or decision against which appeal is made, is temporarily suspended, unless the delay thereby caused is considered contrary to the public interests.

The term "supervising" or "superintending office," refers to the governor of the prefecture, or the prefectural council, as the case may be, and the Minister for Home Affairs. It is the duty of the supervising office to see that the administration of the city is conducted properly, and in the manner most conducive to the common weal. If the city assembly refuses to include in the estimates, or to give special sanction to, disbursements that it is bound by law, or by the lawful order of a supervising office, to make, the governor may add the necessary sum to the estimates, or cause the special payment to be made. The city assembly has in such case the right to appeal to the administrative court. If the city assembly or council omit to discuss and decide motions which ought to be discussed and decided by them, the prefectural council does so instead.

The Minister for Home Affairs may, at any time, cause the city assembly to be dissolved; in such case a fresh election must be held within three months. Until the meeting of the new assembly, the prefectural council decides any pressing question that may arise.

In the following matters the consent of the Minister for Home Affairs is necessary before a resolution of the city assembly can be put into force:—

1. The making or alteration of by-laws. (The Imperial consent is also necessary in this case.)
2. The sale, transfer, mortgage, exchange or alteration (to any large extent) of city property important as being connected with the fine arts, learning or accomplishments, or from historical associations.

In the following matters the consent of both the Minister for Home Affairs and the Minister for Finance is necessary:—

1. The undertaking of new or increased monetary burdens by the city, unless the discharge of the same is to be completed within three years.
2. The levying or increase of, or making of alterations in, special municipal taxes, rents and fees.
3. The levying of municipal taxes additional to direct national taxes, where the rate in the case of land tax exceeds one-seventh, and in the case of other taxes exceeds fifty per cent., of the rate at which national tax is paid.
4. The levying of municipal taxes supplementary to indirect national taxes.
5. The decision as to disbursements to be made against money given as a subsidy by a Government office, in accordance with law or Imperial decree.

In the following matters the consent of the prefectural council is necessary to resolutions of the city assembly:—

1. The making and alteration of rules relating to municipal works and plant.
2. All dealings with city capital (i.e. immovable property, and deposits of money or grain, &c.)
3. Sale, transfer or mortgage of real property belonging to the city.
4. Alterations in the rules relating to the special use of city property by individuals.
5. The giving of any kind of security or guarantee.

6. The imposing on the citizens of new obligations, to extend beyond a period of five years, which it is not their duty to accept by law or Imperial decree.

7. The imposition of taxes additional to national or prefectural taxes, but which are not levied at uniform rates.

8. The meeting of expenses by means of taxes levied on individual persons or on particular wards.

9. The levying of forced labour and contributions, the assessment of which is not uniform with that of direct city taxes.

DISCIPLINARY PUNISHMENT.

The governor of the prefecture possesses the power of inflicting disciplinary punishment on the mayor, vice-mayor, members of the council and committees, heads of wards, and all other city officials. Punishments may take the form of a reprimand, the infliction of a fine of not more than twenty-five yen, or dismissal. Appeals against the governor's decisions may be made to the administrative court. When punishment is inflicted by the city council, appeal lies in the first instance to the governor, then to the court.

A city official may be dismissed for repeated breaches of discipline, for wasting public money, or for neglect of duty. Such dismissal entails the forfeiture of any pension to which he may be entitled. Decisions with reference to the dismissal of a mayor must be reported to the Emperor. While a case is under consideration, the offender's salary may be stopped, or he may be suspended from the performance of his duties.

If a city official, by neglecting his duties, or exceeding his powers, cause pecuniary loss to the city, the prefectural council may order him to make good such loss. Appeal lies to the administrative court, and must be made within seven days. The goods of the offender may be temporarily seized as security for payment of the money.

URBAN PREFECTURES.

During the year 1898 the special rules which had previously existed with regard to the municipal affairs of the three cities of Tokyo, Kyoto and Osaka were abolished, and at the same time the following modifications were made in the city regulations as applied to them:—

The wards being continued as heretofore are also to be electoral districts for the city assembly. By resolution of the city assembly, a revenue officer may be appointed to any ward; such officer to transact financial business of the ward under the orders of the city council. Heads of wards take their instruction from the mayor, council or revenue officer of the city, and may be entrusted with the transaction of city business (in addition to ward business) within the limits of their wards. A ward revenue officer may assist in the transaction of city financial business within the limits of his ward. The mayor may, if approved by the superintending office, distribute amongst the heads of wards the transaction of business with which he is specially charged by law: *e.g.*, work in connection with relief of shipwrecked persons, &c.

It may be as well to add that, though the word *fu* is sometimes translated as "Imperial city," the better rendering is "urban prefecture," and that there is practically no difference between the administration of *fu* and *ken*. She latter term should, strictly speaking, be translated "rural prefecture."

For instance, a careful distinction should be drawn between Osaka *fu* and Osaka *shi*. The former is a prefecture, containing, in addition to the cities of Osaka and Sakai, nine *gun* or rural districts, whilst Osaka *shi* is Osaka city, pure and simple. As regards size, there is little to choose between a *fu* and a small *ken*.

THE ADMINISTRATION OF THE CITY OF KOBE.

IN order to show by a practical example the manner in which the administration of a Japanese city is carried on, I append a short account of the Municipal affairs of Kobe, which may be taken as an excellent type of a thriving Japanese city.

ASSEMBLY.

In 1888, when the city regulations were put into force, Kobe (which includes Hyogo) was divided into four electoral wards, with a total of thirty-six representatives. In 1895, the number of representatives was increased to thirty-nine, but the wards remained unchanged. It may be noticed that the electoral wards are distinct from the administrative wards, which will be mentioned later on.

The following table shows the particulars of the latest general election, which took place in 1898, when twenty members retired after having served their period of six years. The population of Kobe then amounted to 183,065; and vacancies occurred in various classes in all four districts:—

GENERAL ELECTION OF 1898.

Electoral district.	Class.	No. of vacancies.	No. of candidates.	No. of persons possessing voters' rights.	No. of persons actually voting.
No. 1 ...	1st	1	2	10	10
	2nd	1	2	40	36
No. 2 ...	2nd	2	4	122	101
	3rd	2	4	750	534
No. 3 ...	1st	2	4	19	14
	3rd	3	7	485	330
No. 4 ...	1st	3	3	1	1
	2nd	4	7	64	56
	3rd	2	5	1,479	695

Of the successful candidates at the above election, eight belonged to the Progressive Party (*Shimpoto*), six to the Radicals (*Jiyuto*), and six were non-political or independent. Of the unsuccessful candidates, five were Progressives, seven Radicals, and six non-political. There was only one case, that of the second class in the fourth ward, in which the contest was wholly non-political. In the case of the first class of the fourth ward, one voter had to elect three representatives. He distributed his favours impartially, choosing one Progressive, one Radical and one Independent.

The members of the Assembly are almost entirely merchants and shopkeepers; several of them have held their seats since 1888.

The election of the chairman and vice-chairman is always political; at present the Progressives are in a majority, and a Progressive chairman is the result.

Meetings of the Assembly are usually held monthly, unless there is any pressing matter to be discussed.

The City Council numbers six members, mostly well-to-do merchants. Among them is a banker.

The present Mayor of Kobe has held office since the City Regulations came into force in 1888; previously to that, he was Mayor of Kobe town (*ku*).

Until last year there was only one Assistant Mayor; but it being considered advisable, in view of the approaching operation of the new Treaties, to have an official well acquainted with law, a second Assistant Mayor was appointed, in the person of a gentleman who is a graduate of the College of Jurisprudence in the Imperial University. There are rumours of plans for the appointment of yet another Assistant Mayor, but nothing has yet been decided.

In 1888 Kobe was divided for administrative purposes into four wards; subsequently the number was increased to six, as it remains at the present day. Each ward possesses an Assembly of its own, the number of members ranging from twenty-four to twelve.

At present there appears to be an idea on foot that if the ward property, which is very considerable, could be all transferred to the city, not only would a great deal of expenditure be saved, but the jealousies between people of the different wards would also cease. On the other hand, the question has been mooted as to whether the present foreign Concession cou'd not be made a ward by itself, after the new Treaties come into force. Even if this were done, the officials would presumably have to be Japanese.

The following table shows the number of persons employed in the City Office on the 23rd of February, 1899; and their distribution amongst the various bureaux.

Bureau.	Number of clerks.	No. of employés, servants, etc.	No. of persons specially employed.	Total.
General Affairs	17	12	5	34
Registration	9	15	9	33
Works	9	5	—	14
Taxation	9	18	9	36
Revenue Office	2	1	1	4
Total	46	51	24	121

In addition to the above, there are two engineers employed in the Bureau of Works.

During last year an interpreter was appointed, in view of the approaching enforcement of the new Treaties. I am informed (from an unofficial source) that a good deal of attention is bestowed upon the utterances of the foreign journals in Kobe, and that translations from them are frequently made for the consideration of the authorities.

The following statistics, showing the amount of work transacted during last year, are taken from a local Japanese newspaper.

In the Bureau of General Affairs the correspondence is classed as follows:—

Received:—16,943 petitions, inquiries and reports, 4,643 letters from public offices and schools, 13 secret communications from the Prefectural Office.

Sent:—2,387 petitions forwarded to public offices, 672 dispatches and reports, 19,210 summonses to attend.

In the Bureau of Registration (*Koseki kwa*), 36,487 communications were received from, and 59,063 sent to, public offices during the year. The number of petitions, inquiries and reports received amounted to 90,488; and 13,633 petitions were passed on to other offices; in addition to which 8,983 answers to petitions and reports were sent to various individuals. The number of persons summoned to attend to answer inquiries and for various purposes was 19,249.

In the Bureau of Works, 303 dispatches were sent to, and 579 received from, other offices; 2,739 petitions and reports were received from citizens; and 399 petitions were forwarded to other offices. 542 persons were summoned to attend on various business.

In the Bureau of Taxation 998 dispatches were sent to, and 636 received from public offices. 864 communications were received and transmitted to citizens, and 4,957 were forwarded on behalf of citizens to other offices. 194,015 notices for payment of taxes, assessment orders, and urgency orders were issued; also 55,107 summonses to attend. Communications received included 37,909 petitions, inquiries and reports, 186 instructions, 56 notices as to changes of tax-payers, and 739 reports of employment or discharge of prostitutes. Orders for levying of taxes amounted to 498.

In the revenue officer's bureau, correspondence with public offices included 531 letters sent and 120 received; and 65 persons were summoned to attend.

FINANCE.

I have had some difficulty in obtaining statistics relating to the revenue and expenditure of Kobe City during past years, due to the only records available being those preserved in the archives of the City Office, and it is owing to the courtesy of the authorities there, that I am enabled to produce the following tables.

First I append a table showing the total revenue and expenditure of Kobe City for the years 1889 to 1897 inclusive, and the estimated revenue and expenditure for the years 1898 and 1899.

TABLE SHOWING TOTAL REVENUE AND EXPENDITURE OF KOBE CITY FOR THE YEARS 1889 TO 1897 INCLUSIVE, WITH ESTIMATED REVENUE AND EXPENDITURE FOR YEARS 1898 AND 1899.

	1889.	1890.	1891.	1892.	1893.	1894.	1895.	1896.	1897.	1898. (estimated.)	1899. (estimated.)
	Yen.	Yen.	Yen.	Yen.	Yen.	Yen.	Yen.	Yen.	Yen.	Yen.	Yen.
Revenue	52,654	73,975	89,200	45,068	65,302	85,703	125,302	317,125	309,687	375,663	391,687
Expenditure	47,741	70,964	87,676	41,140	65,302	77,469	91,986	285,366	269,283	375,663	392,189

It will be noticed that the rate of expenditure shows a great increase after the time of the Chinese war; at the same period, a general rise occurred in the price of commodities.

I next give tables showing in detail the estimated and actual revenue and expenditure of the city for the year 1897. Up to the beginning of this year, the yearly financial reports only were printed, while the estimates were written by hand, but now both reports and estimates are printed. Consequently full details of the estimates for 1898 were not easily forthcoming, but I have obtained, for comparative purposes, the main points which are given in the table below. The financial report for 1898 will not be published till June of this year. The estimates for 1899 are as given in the columns of the local Japanese newspaper.

TABLE SHOWING DETAILS OF THE ESTIMATED AND ACTUAL REVENUE OF KOBE CITY FOR THE YEAR 1897, AND OF THE ESTIMATED REVENUE FOR THE YEARS 1898 AND 1899.

	1897. Estimated. Yen.	1897. Actual. Yen.	1898. Estimated. Yen.	1899. Estimated. Yen.
1. Rents and fees:—				
Rent of houses on embankment and in park	880	1,717	—	—
Rent of village roads	350	307	—	—
Fees—on employment and dismissal of seamen	2,500	3,033	—	—
„ —urgency order for payment of taxes	150	291	—	—
Total	3,880	5,348	5,066	6,978
2. Assistance from national taxes	4,600	4,690	6,000	6,480
3. Miscellaneous:—				
Sale of old timber	200	156	—	—
„ „ useless material	130	86	—	—
„ „ useless land	2,802	2,802	—	—
Sundry	2,409	3,862	—	—
Total	5,541	6,906	5,580	2,470
4. Brought forward from last year	31,759	31,759	40,405	11,342

5. City taxes:—				
Additional land tax	19,383	19,609	—	—
„ income tax	12,150	12,487	—	—
„ business tax	43,650	49,513	—	—
(Special) Business tax	11,731	18,589	—	—
„ Miscellaneous taxes	61,762	76,852	—	—
„ House tax	44,901	46,812	—	—
„ *Buichizei*	23,000	24,554	—	—
Total	216,577	248,416	316,496	364,417
6. Public loan	21,582	12,568	2,166	—
Grand Total	283,939	309,687	375,663	391,687

TABLE SHOWING DETAILS OF THE ESTIMATED AND ACTUAL EXPENDITURE OF KOBE CITY FOR THE YEAR 1897, AND OF THE ESTIMATED EXPENDITURE FOR THE YEARS 1898 AND 1899.

	1897. Estimated. Yen.	1897. Actual. Yen.	1898. Estimated. Yen.	1899. Estimated. Yen.
I.—Ordinary Expenditure.				
1. Office expenses:—				
Mayor's salary	1,800	1,800	—	—
Assistant mayor's salary	800	800	—	—
Clerks' salaries	10,608	9,092	—	—
Employés' salaries	6,182	6,260	—	—
Revenue officer's salary	360	360	—	—
Servants' wages	3,758	3,472	—	—
Travelling expenses	2,704	3,733	—	—
Stationery, printing, etc.	3,857	5,553	—	—
Repairs	465	603	—	—
Total	30,534	31,673	40,046	51,854
2. Assembly expenses:—				
Members' expenses	1,022	426	—	—
Clerk's salary	18	—	—	—
Printing	150	220	—	—
Sundries	35	24	—	—
Total	1,225	670	1,945	1,945
3. Public works:—				
Repair of roads, bridges, etc.	22,367	22,444	—	—
„ of embankments	3,550	3,542	—	—
Wages	3,623	3,582	—	—
Other	2,106	2,141	—	—
Total	31,646	31,709	30,191	51,392
4. Sanitary expenses	2,221	4,099	2,722	3,517
5. Relief expenses (*kiujohi*)	300	210	300	300
6. Precautionary expenses (against fire, etc.):—				
Wages	3,593	4,233	—	—
Machinery, tools, etc.	645	729	—	—
Other	395	346	—	—
Total	4,633	5,308	4,568	5,824

7. Encouragement of business	225	175	237	112
8. Taxes and burdens	119	119	173,626	207,928
9. Sundry disbursements	156	1,104	2,537	1,037
10. Reserve for emergencies	6,563		3,097	2,000
11. City property expenses	2,802	2,802	2,500	1,000
12. Prefectural expenses	68,907	68,907	included under No. 8 above	included under No. 8 above
Total Ordinary Expenditure	149,331	146,776	261,769	326,909
II.—Special Expenditure.				
1. Public loan expenses:—				
Repayment of loans	57,682	58,909	—	—
Interest on loans	15,060	11,047	—	—
Total	72,742	69,956	82,708	53,026
2. Sanitary expenses	4,163	4,144	4,912	-
3. Public works	25,988	20,050	6,390	2,667
4. Harbour survey expenses	25,976	22,675	19,884	6,587
5. Education	2,732	2,671	—	—
6. Encouragement of business (Marine Products Exhibition)	700	700	—	3,000
7. Official property bought from Government	2,309	2,309	—	—
Total Special Expenditure	134,610	122,505	113,894	65,280
Grand Total	283,941	269,281	375,663	392,189

I may note that since 1897 the Mayor's salary has been increased to 2,200 *yen* per annum. Of the two Assistant Mayors, one receives 1,200 *yen* and the other 1,000 *yen*.

WARD FINANCE.

The following tables show details of the aggregate estimated and actual revenue and expenditure of the six wards of Kobe for the year 1897, and the estimated revenue and expenditure for the year 1898. The amounts for the various wards differ very considerably, in proof of which I may mention that the total revenue of Kobe Ward, the richest, amounted in 1897 to *yen* 53,955, while that of Minato Ward, the poorest, only reached *yen* 11,120. The figures here given I obtained from the City Office, and as the totals for the six wards only were given, I reproduce them in the same form.

TABLE SHOWING DETAILS OF THE AGGREGATE ESTIMATED AND ACTUAL REVENUE OF THE SIX WARDS OF KOBE FOR THE YEAR 1897, AND OF THE AGGREGATE ESTIMATED REVENUE FOR THE YEAR 1898.

	1897. Estimated. Yen.	1897. Actual. Yen.	1898. Estimated. Yen.
Income derived from ward property	8,948	10,021	10,173
Rents and fees	351	342	342
Miscellaneous	131,026	126,749	46,847
Brought forward from last year	21,798	21,661	17,406
City Taxes	51,827	54,158	63,936
Contributions	3,760	1,035	60,491
Assistance from national treasury	450	375	800
Public loans	65,984	35,951	69,250
Total	284,144	250,292	269,245

TABLE SHOWING DETAILS OF THE AGGREGATE ESTIMATED AND ACTUAL EXPENDITURE OF THE SIX WARDS OF KOBE FOR THE YEAR 1897, AND OF THE AGGREGATE ESTIMATED EXPENDITURE FOR THE YEAR 1898.

	1897. Estimated. Yen.	1897. Actual. Yen.	1898. Estimated. Yen.
I.—Ordinary expenditure.			
Assembly expenses	464	520	693
Expenses incurred in preservation of ward property	1,052	1,013	1,185
Taxes, etc.	904	958	1,012
Education	68,214	62,640	82,135
Laid aside as capital	2,810	2,810	6,792
Repairs	60	198	60
Cemetery expenses	298	283	256
Emergencies	12,032	—	17,063
Miscellaneous	6	316	21
Total Ordinary Expenditure	85,840	68,738	109,217
II.—Special expenditure.			
Forest examination	100	91	100
Loan expenses (interest and repayment)	32,366	30,507	38,098
Educational (building, repairs, etc.)	165,838	133,662	114,699
Reclamation of sea shore	—	—	5,567
Purchase of land	—	—	2,013
Total Special Expenditure	198,304	164,260	160,477
Grand Total	284,144	232,998	269,694

TAXES.

Finally, I intend to give some account of the City taxes at present levied in Kobe. The subject is an intricate one, and it is necessary at times to generalise, but care has been taken to omit nothing that is likely to affect foreigners after the coming into operation of the New Treaties. At the same time it must be borne in mind that the rates of these taxes may be altered at any time by the City Assembly, on obtaining the consent of the proper authorities; and that the tendency at the present moment is distinctly in the direction of increased taxation.

The City "additional" taxes, assessed at proportionate rates to, and upon the same persons as, the national taxes, are levied as follows:—

1. Land Tax: levied at the rate of 46 sen 4 rin for, and in addition to, every yen of national Land Tax paid. Amount realised in 1897 reached 19,609 yen.
2. Income Tax: at rate of 45 per cent. of national tax, which is estimated to amount in Kobe to about 30,600 yen.
3. Business Tax: at rate of 50 per cent. of national tax, which is estimated to amount in Kobe to about 130,000 yen.

The special City taxes comprise the following:—
1. Business Tax.
2. Miscellaneous Taxes (*zasshuzei*).
3. House Tax.
4. *Buichizei* (a tax levied on sales and transfers of land or houses, at rate of 1 per cent. of the price, estimated to bring in about 23,000 yen).

With regard to the BUSINESS TAX, it may first be noticed that any person who intends to carry on a trade or business within the City must report the fact to the City Authorities, and obtain a licence (*kansatsu*). A recent "raid" by the City officials is said to have disclosed the fact that of the sixteen thousand persons, carrying on business in Kobe, six thousand were without licences. There are bye-laws relating to the reporting of amount of income derived from business, and other points in connection with the tax, for infractions of which a fine of not more than 1 yen 95 sen, and not less than 25 sen, may be imposed.

Business Tax is levied on the following:—

(1) Trades, including merchants, wholesale and retail, curio-dealers; hotel and lodging-house keepers, forwarding agencies, pawn-brokers, money-lenders, money-changers, and the like.

Tax is levied according to yearly income realised, ranging from the first class—incomes of 900 yen or more—with a tax of 7 yen 60 sen per annum, increasing 1 yen 50 sen in tax for every 100 yen in income, down to the twelfth class—incomes of 30 yen—with a yearly tax of 1 yen.

(2) Industries, including factories, carpenters, stone-masons, plasterers, joiners, blacksmiths, printers, photographers and the like.

Tax is levied according to yearly income realised, ranging from first class—incomes of 500 yen and upwards—with a tax of 4 yen 80 sen, increasing at rate of 1 yen in tax for 100 yen in income, down to eighth class—incomes of 30 yen—with a tax of 60 sen.

The total amount brought in by the Business Tax in 1897 amounted to yen 18,589.

MISCELLANEOUS TAXES include the following:—

Tax levied on restaurants, tea-houses, eating-houses, &c., at rates varying from first class—incomes of 1,000 yen—with tax of 15 yen per annum, increasing at rate of 2 yen in tax for every 100 yen in income, down to seventh class—yearly income of 30 yen—with tax of 1 yen 50 sen.

Tax levied on bath-houses (including medicinal baths), ranging from first class, with tax of 15 yen on incomes of 1,000 yen, increasing 2 yen for every 100 yen in income, down to ninth class, with tax of 1 yen 50 sen on incomes of 30 yen.

Tax levied on hair-dressers, barbers, &c., ranging from first class, with tax of 12 yen on incomes of 1,000 yen, increasing at rate of 1 yen 50 sen in tax for every 100 yen in income, down to ninth class, with tax of 1 yen on incomes of 30 yen.

Tax on teachers of the amusing arts, 4 yen 50 sen a year each person.

Tax on performers of the amusing arts, 6 yen a year on persons of over 15 years of age, 3 yen on those under.

Tax on wrestlers, ranging, according to class, from 6 to 2 yen a year.

Tax on actors, ranging from 8 to 2 yen a year.

Taxes on horses; riding horse, for personal use, 6 yen a year; for employment in business, 3 yen; horse for draught purposes, 2 yen.

Tax on water-wheels, ranging from 6 yen to 13 sen, according to mode of use.

Taxes on ships: small Japanese boats of less than 3 ken (about 18 feet) in length, 50 sen a year; for every additional ken, 10 sen extra; or for every koku (2½ piculs) above 50 koku of lading, two sen per koku. Foreign-style sailing vessels, 10 sen for every ton; steamboats, 15 sen for every ton.

Taxes on wheeled vehicles; for carriages, two horses, 6 yen a year, one horse 4 yen; for carts drawn by horses, 4 yen a year; for a double *jinrikisha*, 3 yen, for a single *jinrikisha*, 1 yen 80 sen a year; for hand carts, 3 yen to 1 yen a year; for bicycles, if for private use, 3 yen, if kept for hire, 1 yen 50 sen a year.

Tax on machinery driven by steam, 1 yen 30 sen per year for each horse-power.

Tax on *yose* (public halls for entertainments, story telling, etc.), from 6 to 3 yen, according to size.

Tax on singing-girls, of over twelve years of age, 4 yen 50 sen per month; if under twelve years of age, 2 yen 25 sen per month.

Tax on theatres, 10 per cent. of profits.

Tax on pleasure booths,—fixed, 7 yen 50 sen per month; special, 50 sen per day.

Tax on slaughter of animals; cow, 60 sen; calf, 30 sen; pig, 30 sen.

The above include all the important taxes levied under the heading of "Miscellaneous." The total amount of revenue rising from this source in 1897 reached yen 76,852.

HOUSE TAX is levied upon a rather complicated system, the rate depending upon the size of the house, the material of which it is constructed, and the assessed value of the ground on which it stands. House Tax is paid not only to the city, but also to the particular ward in which the house is situated.

Tax is paid in advance every six months. At the beginning of the financial year, the City Assembly fixes the amount of the unit on which taxation is to be based during the ensuing year for each period of six months. The unit for each ward is fixed by the Ward Assembly. Under special circumstances the Assembly may increase the amount of the unit during the year, on obtaining the consent of the proper authorities.

As regards construction, the proportion of tsubo on which the tax is charged varies as the house is constructed of brick or wood. If the house be single-storied, and built of stone or brick, tax is assessed as against one and a half tsubo for every tsubo of actual extent. If the house have an upper story, tax is further paid on the upper story, but is only assessed as against 1 tsubo for every tsubo of actual extent. In the case of wooden houses, tax is paid on every tsubo of actual extent; in the case of two-storied wooden houses, tax is further paid on the upper story at the rate of half a tsubo for every tsubo of actual extent.

In deciding the rate of assessment according to value of the land on which the house is situated, the division into classes of land for purposes of assessment of national Land Tax is taken as a basis. These classes, two hundred in number, are grouped together to form twenty-nine classes for assessment of House Tax. A house on land of the first class pays tax at the rate of fifteen times the unit of taxation, a house on land of the second class pays tax at the rate of fourteen and a half times the unit; down to the twenty-ninth class, where the unit remains unchanged.

Kobe Ward, being in the most important part of the city, has the highest rated houses; in the Soto Ward, the highest rated houses are in the ninth class, at a rate of eleven times the unit; in the Sosei, the highest are the tenth class, at the rate of ten and a half times the unit. In the Minato, Fukini, and Hayashida Wards, the amount of the unit itself only is charged.

I append a table showing the amount of the unit of taxation for Kobe City and its various wards from the years 1893 to 1898, inclusive. Amounts are given in sen and decimals thereof.

TABLE SHOWING AMOUNT OF THE UNIT OF TAXATION FOR THE PURPOSE OF ASSESSMENT OF HOUSE TAX IN KOBE AND ITS WARDS FOR THE YEARS 1893 TO 1898.

	1893.		1894.		1895.		1896.		1897.		1898.	
	1st half.	2nd half.	1st half.	2nd half.	1st half.	2nd half.	1st half.	2nd half.	1st half.	2nd half.	1st half.	2nd half.
Kobe City	.1755	.31	.1	.2815	.1	.1	.1	.1	1.1	1.24	1.2	2.0282347
Kobe Ward	.25	.25	.24	.87	.5865	.5865	.5	1.73	1.05	1.05	.95	.95
Fukini "	.88965	1.12765	1.4635	1.4635	1.5165	1.5165	2.	4.51	4.4	4.4	1.6	1.6
Soto "	.5	.5	.6	1.65	1.035	1.035	1.225	1.672628	1.3	1.3	1.5	1.5
Sosei "	.3325	.3325	.5685	.5685	.514	.514	.865	1.415	1.05	1.05	1.1	1.8
Hayashida Ward	—	—	—	—	—	—	5.6	3.85	3.25	3.25	4.0	4.0
Minato Ward	—	—	—	—	—	—	2.35	2.35	1.5	1.5	4.0	4.0

The Hayashida and Minato Wards only came into existence in the year 1896. It may be pointed out that, though in these two wards the rate of the unit appears comparatively high, nevertheless, owing to the low assessment of the land, the amount of tax paid is really smaller than in the other wards.

It will be noticed that the rate has increased a good deal of late years, especially the City rate, which shows a leap from a total of 2 rin in 1896 to 2 sen 3.4 rin in 1897, and a further increase to over 3 sen for the year 1898.

The amount of revenue obtained from the House Tax in 1897 reached in Kobe City yen 46,812, in Kobe Ward, the highest, yen 16,332, and in Minato Ward the lowest, yen 522.

WARD TAXES.

In addition to the above-mentioned special House Tax, the only other tax levied by wards specially is an additional Land Tax, at the rate of five per cent. of the amount of national Land Tax paid. The rate appears to be the same for all six wards. The amount raised by the tax in 1897 amounted in Kobe Ward to yen 858, and in Minato Ward to yen 95 only. Ward taxes are collected together with, and at the same time as the City taxes, and the amounts are distributed afterwards.

It seems probable that coming years will see a still further increase of taxation. Already a plan for raising the rate of Miscellaneous Taxes has been brought forward; but before any alteration can be made, the consent of the Ministers for Home Affairs and Finance is necessary, as pointed out in the former part of this report.

CONCLUDING REMARKS.

Recently there has been further talk of an increase in the number of clerks employed in the City Office; and before the New Treaties come into force, it is likely that two or more interpreters will be employed, in addition to the one already appointed. But there is a very pressing need for better accommodation, and it is to be hoped that a new office will be built as soon as funds permit—an improvement that would be of much more practical use than the construction of an official residence for the Mayor, which latter design has been a great deal discussed. The City Office is still a young institution, and as time goes on, experience will suggest improvements. It is to be hoped, also, that an attempt will be made to prevent, as far as possible, the vexatious delays which are sometimes discernible in the transaction of business at the lesser public offices in Kobe.

Printed by Libri Plureos GmbH in Hamburg, Germany